SAVING THE PLANET THROUGH GREEN ENERGY

FOSSIL FUELS

COLIN GRADY

Enslow Publishing
101 W. 23rd Street
Suite 240
New York, NY 10011
USA

enslow.com

Published in 2017 by Enslow Publishing, LLC.
101 W. 23rd Street, Suite 240, New York, NY 10011

Library of Congress Cataloging-in-Publication Data
Names: Grady, Colin, author.
Title: Fossil fuels / Colin Grady.
Description: New York, NY : Enslow Publishing, 2017. | Series: Saving the planet through green energy | Audience: Ages 8+. | Audience: Grades 4-6. | Includes bibliographical references and index.
Identifiers: LCCN 2016021726| ISBN 9780766082786 (library bound) | ISBN 9780766082762 (pbk.) | ISBN 9780766082779 (6-pack)
Subjects: LCSH: Fossil fuels—Juvenile literature. | Natural resources—Juvenile literature. | Fossil fuels—Environmental aspects—Juvenile literature.
Classification: LCC TP318.3 .G678 2017 | DDC 333.8/2—dc23
LC record available at https://lccn.loc.gov/2016021726

Printed in China

To Our Readers: We have done our best to make sure all website addresses in this book were active and appropriate when we went to press. However, the author and the publisher have no control over and assume no liability for the material available on those websites or on any websites they may link to. Any comments or suggestions can be sent by e-mail to customerservice@enslow.com.

Portions of this book originally appeared in the book *Fossil Fuels: Buried in the Earth* by Amy S. Hansen.

Photo Credits: Cover, p. 1 Thaiview/Shutterstock.com (pumpjacks); Mad Dog/Shutterstock.com (series logo and chapter openers); p. 6 wavebreakmedia/Shutterstock.com; p. 7 Kodda/Shutterstock.com; p. 9 hiroshi teshigawara/Shutterstock.com; p. 10 Ty Wright/Bloomberg/Getty Images; p. 11 abutyrin/Shutterstock.com; p. 15 hans engbers/Shutterstock.com; p. 16 zhangyang13576997233/Shutterstock.com; p. 18 Benjamin Lowy/Getty Images News/Getty Images; p. 19 Vitoriano Junior/Shutterstock.com; p. 21 Mat Hayward/Shuttertock.com; p. 22 Steve Meese/Shutterstock.com.

CONTENTS

WORDS TO KNOW

atmosphere The gases around an object in space. On the earth this is air.

coils Curls.

energy The power to work or to act.

engineers Masters at planning and building engines, machines, roads, and bridges.

fuels Things used to make warmth or power.

gasoline A fuel made from oil. Most cars run on gasoline.

magnets Things that are pulled toward one another by a force called magnetism.

nonrenewable Not able to be replaced once used.

process To treat or change something using a special series of steps.

reflected Thrown back.

United Nations A worldwide group formed to keep peace between nations.

CHAPTER 1

FOSSIL FUELS TODAY

The gasoline that we put into our cars is made from oil, a fossil fuel.

You may have heard the term "fossil fuels," but what exactly are they? Oil, natural gas, and coal are fossil fuels. They are made from long-dead plants and animals. We burn these **fuels** to make heat and electricity. The **gasoline** that powers our cars, buses, trains, and airplanes is made from oil.

In the United States, most of our **energy** comes from fossil fuels. However, fossil fuels take millions of years to form. These fuels are **nonrenewable**. That means that once we use them,

When we burn fossil fuels, we make pollution. This power plant is burning coal.

they are gone forever. Fossil fuels also cause pollution. When they burn they send smoke into our air. When they are taken out of the earth, they cause damage or pollution to the land. Using energy from the sun, water, wind, and the earth's heat are cleaner ways to make power.

CHAPTER 2

TYPES OF FOSSIL FUELS

Oil, natural gas, and coal are fossil fuels that are used every day. Millions of gallons of slippery, liquid oil are pumped from the earth day after day. Most oil is underground, so people must pump it out to use it.

Oil formed from small organisms, or living things, that lived in the seas. After these organisms died, their remains sank. Mud and sand buried them. This weight, and lots of time, changed the remains into oil and natural gas.

DISCOVERY OF OIL

Oil was discovered in Pennsylvania in 1859. At first kerosene was made from the oil. Kerosene was used to the replace whale oil in lamps. In

1908, Henry Ford started selling cars. As people began buying cars, they needed oil to make gasoline. Gasoline was lighter than kerosene and was a better fuel for car engines. Today, oil fuels more than a billion cars around the world!

Oil is the remains of living things that made their home in the oceans long ago. If oil spills on land, it causes damage to animals and habitats.

NATURAL GAS

Just like oil, natural gas formed millions of years ago from small organisms that lived in water. Natural gas is sometimes found alongside oil. Oil fields often have oil on the bottom and natural gas on top. People pump gas out of

Workers build a pipeline to carry natural gas from Colorado to Ohio.

wells and **process** it. This produces natural gas and other liquids. One of the liquids is propane, which is often used in gas grills.

Natural gas cannot be seen or smelled. However, when **engineers** put natural gas into pipes, they add a chemical that smells like rotten eggs. This way, people can smell the gas if the pipes leak.

COAL

Coal is a hard, black rock. Unlike most rocks, though, coal burns. We burn it to make heat and electricity. It has more carbon than any of the fossil fuels. It adds the most carbon dioxide to the air when it burns.

Coal is the most plentiful fossil fuel. After it is dug up, the coal is loaded into trucks that take it to be crushed. That makes it easier to ship and burn.

Coal started forming three hundred million years ago, when the earth was wetter. Coal is made from the remains of plants that grew in the wet ground. When they died, these plants sank into the mud. They became spongy matter called peat. In time, rocks piled up over the peat. Their weight pressed on the peat. This dried the peat out and changed it into coal. We mine, or dig up, coal in many places in the United States and around the world.

FOSSIL FUELS TIMELINE

300 million years ago The earth is warmer and wetter. Fossil fuels start forming.

1765 James Watt invents a new steam engine. It runs on coal and is used mostly to pump water out of mines.

1858–1859 North America's first oil wells are dug in Ontario and Pennsylvania.

1879 Thomas Edison makes the first useful lightbulb. People soon start using lightbulbs and building power plants to make electricity.

1908 Henry Ford's Model T hits the road. This is the first car that most people can afford.

1970 The US government passes the Clean Air Act. Power plants have to start cleaning up their smokestacks. New cars cannot pollute as much.

1997 The **United Nations** agrees to try to slow global warming. The agreement, called the Kyoto Protocol, is signed in Kyoto, Japan.

2000s Clean coal technology focuses on removing or reducing the pollution from the burning of coal in power plants.

2005 The Energy Policy Act of 2005 is passed. It requires the use of more renewable fuels for transportation and new ways to reduce pollution from gasoline and diesel.

2010 BP oil rig in the Gulf of Mexico explodes and causes largest oil spill in US history.

2010 Twenty-nine miners are killed in an underground explosion at the Upper Big Branch Mine in West Virginia. This is the worst mining accident in United States since 1972.

2015 President Barack Obama announces the Clean Power Plan idea, setting the first US limits on the amount of carbon dioxide that can be given off by a power plant.

CHAPTER 3

POWER PLANTS FOR ELECTRICITY

Many sources of energy can be used to make electricity. Wind, water, solar, geothermal, and nuclear power are cleaner energy sources to produce electricity. But it is not possible to power the entire world with these power sources. Although more power plants are being built to use these renewable energy sources, we need fossil fuels to make enough energy for the world.

WHERE DOES ELECTRICITY COME FROM?

Electricity powers the devices in your home, the lights in your school, and the air-conditioning in buildings. Where does it come from? Wires connect a home or building to a power plant that makes electricity.

Most power plants burn coal, oil, or natural gas. The burning fuel heats up water. This turns

Electricity is made at a power plant. Wires carry the electricity to your home. This power plant burns coal for energy.

Some power plants use renewable energy. The blue solar cells at this power plant collect the sun's energy.

the water into steam. The hot steam rises and turns a turbine, or giant wheel. The turbine turns a generator. This is the part of the power plant that actually makes electricity. Inside a generator, there are magnets and **coils** of wire. The generator spins the wires past the **magnets**. That movement makes electricity.

CHAPTER 4

FOSSIL FUELS AND PLANET EARTH

When people burn fossil fuels, they send smoke into the air. The smoke is made of many gases. Some of the gases stay close to the ground and make it hard to breathe. Other gases make it into the **atmosphere**. This causes polluted rain, which hurts plants and animals.

Fossil fuels also pollute as they are taken out of the ground. Oil sometimes spills and makes a gooey mess. Coal dust blows away and poisons streams and rivers. The machines that dig up coal sometimes dig up forests as well. Pollution happens even when people are very careful.

GLOBAL WARMING

The sun sends energy to Earth. Much of this energy is **reflected** back into space. Some energy gets trapped by the atmosphere, though. This keeps Earth just warm enough for living things.

The BP oil spill was a disaster in the Gulf of Mexico in 2010. Oil washed up on the shore, covering the sandy beaches and wildlife.

When we burn fossil fuels, we change that. Burning fossil fuels creates gases that end up in the atmosphere. The gases trap more of the sun's energy inside Earth's atmosphere. That causes Earth to warm up quickly. This is called global warming. It causes ice and snow to melt faster. It also means some places have stronger storms and other places have fewer storms than before.

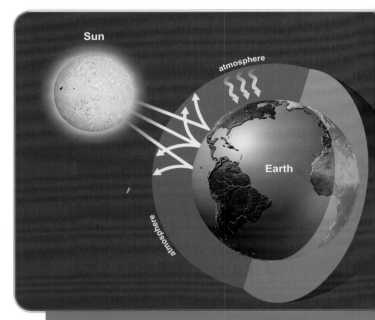

Earth's atmosphere is very good at keeping us warm enough to live. But when pollution gets trapped in the atmosphere, it traps even more heat. This makes the planet warmer and causes changes in our weather.

CHAPTER 5

FOSSIL FUELS FOREVER?

Will we start using less energy before we run out of fossil fuels? That would take a lot of change. Many people like having a car. Most cars run on gasoline. Once a car burns gasoline, the gasoline is gone. We cannot get it back again. People also want electricity. Burning fossil fuels is an easy way to make electricity and heat. We also use fossil fuels to make plastics, nylon clothes, and other important things. However, these fuels pollute our world and will be used up over time.

Scientists are finding new ways to burn fossil fuels in power plants. This would cause less pollution. It would also mean that we would need less of the fuels. This is a good first step.

CLEANER ENERGY

In 2015, 81 percent of the energy used in the United States came from fossil fuels. That is less than it used to be, but we still have work to do. Scientists are finding ways to use the energy from inside the earth and from the sun. Water, wind, and nuclear reactions can also be used. This way we will need less energy from fossil fuels.

If we begin to use cleaner energy to make the electricity we all use, it will be better for our health and our planet.

Wind is a renewable energy source. This wind farm has a row of large wind turbines. The turbines spin and make electricity.

WILL FOSSIL FUELS LAST?

How long fossil fuels last depends on how we use them. At the rate we are going, oil and natural gas may last for about fifty more years. Scientists think coal could last for about two hundred more years, but it makes much more pollution than oil and natural gas, and especially more than solar power, wind power, and hydropower. We must find other ways to fuel our world that are plentiful, renewable, and cleaner!

FURTHER READING

BOOKS

Centore, Michael. *Renewable Energy*. Broomall, PA: Mason Crest, 2015.

Einspruch, Andrew. *What Is Energy?* New York, NY: PowerKids Press, 2014.

Kopp, Megan. *Living in a Sustainable Way: Green Communities.* New York, NY: Crabtree Publishing Co., 2016.

Otfinoski, Steven. *Wind, Solar, and Geothermal Power: From Concept to Consumer.* New York, NY: Children's Press, 2016.

Sneideman, Joshua. *Renewable Energy: Discover the Fuel of the Future with 20 Projects.* White River Junction, VT: Nomad Press, 2016.

Spilsbury, Richard. *Energy.* Chicago, IL: Capstone Press, 2014.

WEBSITES

Energy Star Kids
energystar.gov/index.cfm?c=kids.kids_index
Learn more facts about energy and how you can save energy and help the planet.

NASA's Climate Kids: Energy
climatekids.nasa.gov/menu/energy
Lots of fun facts and links about energy.

US Energy Information Administration
eia.gov/kids
Read about the history of energy, get facts about the types of energy, learn tips to save energy, and link to games and activities.

INDEX